THE WISDOM OF SAINT GERMAIN

Messages of Love from the Spiritual Master

Dear Elinor —

I feel so honored to know you & to have worked with your talents which God has blessed to much. It is your execution of Saint Germain's face that all readers will see first. Thank you dear heart. Thank you.

Love always,
Philip

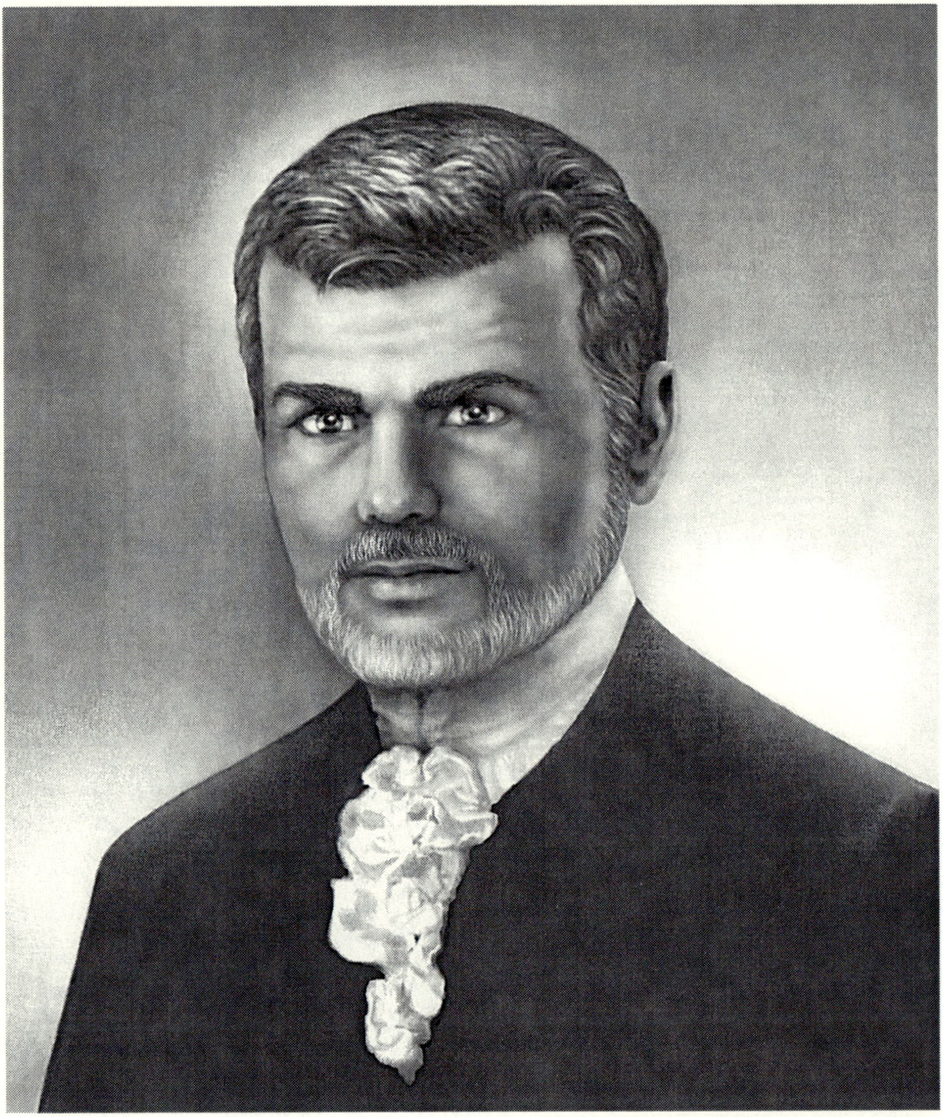

Also from Mastery Press:

The Gift of Mediumship

A Legacy of Love
Volume One: The Return to Mount Shasta and Beyond

To Master Self is to Master Life

Awaken the Sleeping Giant

A Wanderer in the Spirit Lands

THE WISDOM OF SAINT GERMAIN

Messages of Love from the Spiritual Master

As Channeled Through the
Mediumship of Philip Burley

Mastery Press

Phoenix, Arizona

Acknowledgments

While it took a number of people to bring this book into existence, including Saint Germain, I want to acknowledge most especially my right hand helper and assistant Lynn Mathers:

Thank you, Lynn, for your dedication in the preparation of *The Wisdom of Saint Germain* quotes that went out to our mailing list like clockwork each week for one year. Without your capable assistance, bringing Saint Germain's precious words to the world could never have been accomplished.

Contents

Preface	xiii
Traveling the River of Life	1
We All Have Problems	3
The Highest Truth Is Love	5
Stay in the Light of Your Life	7
You Were Born out of Love	9
Writing and Following Your Book of Life	11
Live Now	13
God Within and We in Spirit Are Ever with You	15
This Life Is *All* about Returning to God	17
Focusing upon God Within	19
Why Surrender?	21
The Purpose and Goal of Spiritual Practice	23
On Marriage	25
Spiritual Ascension: Climbing the Mountain of Life	27
Knowing Yourself	29
God's Love for His Creation	31
Your Light Essence	33
When Anchored in God	35
All Work Is Holy	37
The Magnificent Reality of Self	39
For the Love of God I Come	41
Loving Servants	43
Finding God	45
What Is Self-Mastery?	47

Why Should You Develop Your Spiritual Abilities?................ 49
Patience... 51
You Are Love Itself....................................... 53
Put Your Spiritual Life First.............................. 55
God Is Your Beloved...................................... 57
We Are All Masters....................................... 59
I Am Worried Most about My Oldest Son 61
In Awe We Worship God, and He Responds in Love and Gratitude .. 63
Spend Time on the Inner Path 65
What Is Life without Suffering............................ 67
Fulfilling the Ideal of Marriage........................... 69
Why I Am Called a Master................................ 71
The Individual Is Most Precious to God 73
Jesus: A Supreme Example of Self-Transformation 75
Do That Which Edifies the Soul........................... 77
On Aging.. 79
The More We Serve, the More We Love 81
True Enlightenment...................................... 83
The Force of Goodness behind All of Creation 85
Focus on Eternal Values.................................. 87
Inner Reflection Is Crucial............................... 89
Channeling: A Means to the Truth......................... 91
You Draw to Yourself What You Are 93
Your Life on Earth Is Very Precious 95
Your Transformation through Positive Thinking.............. 97
By Serving Others, We Parent Them........................ 99
Accepting Yourself as You Are............................. 101
Meditation: The Great Journey Inward to Find Your True
    Self and God....................................... 103
About Philip Burley...................................... 105
About Saint Germain..................................... 107
Sources.. 109

Preface

There are wisdom teachings in the world from innumerable spiritual masters, Saint Germain among them. Within this book are timeless and inspiring words of Saint Germain, passages drawn from a decade of his speaking to audiences in person, on the radio, or in individual spiritual readings. They were made public one by one during 2008 through a weekly electronic mailing entitled *The Wisdom of Saint Germain*.

The response was immediate and enthusiastic, with readers forwarding the quotes to friends and contacts around the world. Many wrote saying how timely a particular quote was for their lives or how helpful a quote had been in answering a life-long question. One woman summed up the thoughts and feelings, perhaps of many, when she wrote, "I love Saint Germain. His words of wisdom are like finding an oasis in a desert."

I have been a channel for Saint Germain for over twenty-one years; and in all this time, I too have been inspired and touched by his words. I can take no credit other than being in place and serving as a vessel that he uses to speak through to those on earth who are prepared and open to receive his wisdom.

The reader will readily recognize the universality of the master's words, as they go simply and directly to the core of the human heart. Saint Germain has the ability, through centuries of experience, to touch us in a way that seems to say, "I know you very well, even better than you know yourself, and I love you because you are you."

Without either condescending or judging, this compassionate and eloquent master helps us correct and heighten our spiritual understanding, pointing the way to higher and higher truth. His goal: that we may find river, nor are you in the boat, because you have flowed into the ocean of life. You then exist in the very presence of God. This whole journey is for one purpose: to wind up in the ocean of God where you experience limitless love, limitless life, and you know that you *are* God.

I do not seek to distract you by being poetic, but rather to say to you: Learn to flow with life. Know that there are no accidents on this river. Whether you find yourself in a safe harbor, in turbulent waters, or in placid waters, it is all God carrying you along. God knows how to flow, how to carry you, and when to bring you home.

Throughout the balance of your life and in your life's work, keep this river in mind. Trust one hundred percent that you are loved, that you are carried along, and that you will arrive home safely. How do I know about the river of life? I have traveled it myself. I know its bends and twists, its torments and its joys, completely. I also know that one can survive it. From this side, I spend many, many hours whispering into the ears of students on earth saying, "You can do it." And I say it now to you, on this river of life, you can do it. You can do it. You can do it!

We All Have Problems

Among billions of people on earth, rich or poor, educated or not, there is no one without problems. The prideful man may deny that he has problems, but he has them. You may think you would be happy if only this or that problem would disappear from your life; but if it did, you would just have different ones.

When you understand that life is for learning about self, you become humble and seek answers. From the first to the twelfth grade and beyond, people study and take tests to see what they have learned. It is important to study self, because you can apply the answers to resolving problems of your life. All human beings go through this process, whether or not they are aware of it.

Do you think I don't have problems? The process of self-mastery goes on through eternity. In the spirit world, we use the word "opportunity" instead of "problem," because every problem provides an opportunity to learn and grow. If you learn from and overcome a problem, you do not need to recycle through it again. The ideal pattern of life is not to go in circles by repeating the same lessons, but to spiral ever upward. Being grateful for your problem is the first step in resolving it. The essential purpose of any problem is to gain wisdom from it. The more problems we solve, the wiser we become.

Beloved ones, from now on, do not see your problems negatively. Turn your energy around and see them as opportunities. Use each one to go higher spiritually. Those of us called masters have mastered life in this way—day by day, year by year, step by step, and little by little. Sometimes we progress and sometimes we have setbacks. We move forward a tiny or large step until we reach the higher levels of self-realization. If you understand this, you have a principle by which to live, work, and grow. Be grateful for your problems and learn what you can learn from them. Remember: If you didn't have the specific problems you have, you would just have different ones. There are no exceptions.

The Highest Truth Is Love

In the higher levels of the spirit world, there are those who seek to approach God through truth, and this is an authentic path. Indeed, spiritual masters who are good at articulating truth can quote this author or that passage from any number of books; but they may have yet to grow fully in unconditional love. In the spirit world, the master of love is higher than the master of truth. Those who love purely are in the highest of the high realms of heaven. They live the truth.

The difference can be explained like this: You see an old woman crossing the street who drops a bag of oranges, and you rush to her because you know it is the right thing to do. Another person watching the same woman with the same problem dashes to her side without thinking that it is the right thing to do—without thinking at all. That person cannot help but go to the old woman out of love. The highest heavens are filled with those who consciously or unconsciously live the truth by becoming love and acting in love.

The highest truth *is* love. One who loves without having to think about it loves unconditionally. That is the pure, core nature of God. The realm from which I come is that of the love of love, not merely the love of truth, and I am drawn to those who come from that same motive.

Love purely. Love with no motive other than seeing the other person as yourself. See God in others. This will draw the highest spirits to assist you on your path. Examine yourself and you will know where you are in relation to these words.

Stay in the Light of Your Life

When the sun comes out blazingly bright, there are no shadows. When you face the sun, even if there are shadows they will fall behind you and will not be in your view. You will be so enthralled with the light and so centered on it that you will not see anything dark.

There are two ways to take dirty water out of a bucket: You can pour the water out and pour clean water in, or drop so many diamonds in the bucket that the dirty water spills out over the edge until it has been completely replaced by diamonds.

Your darker side has a tendency to keep you locked in, and when you focus there, it becomes magnified and powerful to the point that it will consume your energies. Pay no attention to the darker side of your nature. When you make a mistake, immediately forgive yourself. Do not examine your mistake over and over. Put your mistakes, like the shadows, behind you and turn to face the light. Then the shadows of your life will melt away. Be kind to yourself. Love self as you would love others. Forgive self as you would forgive others. Focus only on that which is good in you, and the good will come to replace any darkness.

When you resist darkness, you engage it. When you wrestle with darkness, you get caught up in it. I am telling you the truth. When the doctor operates on a cancer patient and removes the tumor, he does not spend his time with the tumor. He turns immediately to the patient, keeps his focus on the healthy body, and continues to treat it. This illustrates how to achieve self-mastery.

God lives in you, and God is the light of lights. Be happy about that and celebrate God's presence. You can discover it through positive thinking, positive feeling, and positive action.

If you want to bring God out in you, be positive in all things. If you do as I say, even if you have to be a good actor in the beginning, you will shorten your spiritual walk by many, many miles.

Yes, being a good actor is an effective means of transforming negative energies into positive energies, even if you have to fool yourself. Whether you are happy or not, act happy, and happiness will come out of you. Act this way, and what you seek will come to you faster. This is one of the greatest secrets to the mystery of self-mastery.

You Were Born out of Love

Whether you know it or not, you were born out of love, you live in love, you are always surrounded by love, and you will return to your origins of love. When you think of God, think of love. Always think of love. Where is God? God is intimately and personally in the temple of yourself. For this reason, you have to find and nurture love in yourself first. When you find the love I speak of, you will find your own divinity and its author, whom we call God.

This knowledge, and the knowledge of how to consistently access the love of God within, is the greatest knowledge of all. You cannot buy your awakening to this presence, this love within, with all the treasures of the world. You have to gain it by effort, over time. It is not something separate from you that you must earn. It is the true reality of your eternal, spiritual self.

Trace the origin of this love and light within, and you will be led back to the one and only source of all life in the universe. You will, indeed, find that there are not two—you and God; you will find that there is only one love, only one energy. There is only God.

Writing and Following Your Book of Life

You are where you are because this is your life and your level of spiritual attainment, but there is more ahead and beyond. I am here to encourage you to continue on your path with a great sense of self-responsibility. The fulfillment of the Christ within each one is the consummation of love that takes place at the moment of liberation from all earthly attachments, and this is true for everyone. Your meeting with your soul puts an end to everything past. Each awakened one is placed in the midst of infinite love and light in which all truth is seen, experienced, and known. As arrived masters have testified, in this state, all is seen as one and coming from one, and the individual disappears.

The drama of life is created by you and for you—not the little "you" but the cosmic, infinite You. You use your creative abilities to know yourself, creating all things for your awareness and pleasure. When you awaken to the real You and to the facts that I am giving you now, nothing else will matter. Your entire life will come into clear perspective.

Since You have put your little life on earth into motion, the cosmic You is now manifested in a finite body. What has been started must be finished, just as the author writes not only the beginning and middle of the book but the ending as well. In accordance with the perpetual nature of life, You, the author, have set in motion a story designed with purposes that will manifest only as each chapter unfolds. It is necessary to not stop your course, which has come to be called your dharma, but to let it unfold to the end. You must understand that it is a story—not for your undoing, but for your God-realization and self-realization. All stories conclude with this ending, though on the way it may not appear so.

While you remain attached to being a finite human being, you will be drawn back to earth. Your story may continue on the other side if you have not completed God-realization and self-realization; a direct knowing that you are God, and you are not different from God—the infinite, indivisible, supreme absolute. For you to be completely free from all earthly attachments, this ultimate reality must dawn within your mind and heart. When you awaken to this truth, you will move on to fulfill the purpose and meaning of being a divine and limitless being of love.

Live Now

Many of you think there is a path somewhere that you should be walking or a life's goal that is hidden from you. When you cannot find that path or know that goal, you think that you are lost. But there is no other path or hidden goal; there is only misunderstanding. Even if you feel lost and do not know what direction to go in, *that* is your path. The path of life is *self*, and the path is wherever you find yourself right now, in this moment. If you suddenly come into money, that is your path; and if that money is taken away, that is your path too. The path is what unfolds in the *now*.

The past and the future do not exist except in memory or projection; and the past and the future can take place only in the now. It is only in the many nows that we experience the fulfillment of our lives. Until we learn to live in the now, we cannot find the true path. God who created us is far wiser than you and I; and God, love, or destiny, whatever you call God, is a power greater than you and I. That power is guiding us each moment, in the now, to precisely where we need to be in order to get what we need to get. The things that we need in order to go where we are supposed to go are happening to us *now*.

Many people look back at their lives and say, "If only I had been born with this or that. If only I had done this or that." But know that everything that happens to you is for a purpose. You cannot change the past, and there are absolutely no mistakes or accidents, even though you may think your life should have been different from how it has been. If you die young and go into the spirit world, you will know that it was the intention of your life to pass over when and how you did.

The secret of life is to let go. Drop all of your stories about what should happen, live in the now, and accept reality as it is.

Humanity is dreaming life away by thinking life should be different, but the great secret to life is to learn to live *now*. When we achieve that reality, the golden door to life opens for us, and from then on our life blossoms more and more. Those who have learned to live this way have mastered self. People, things, and situations come to them without their asking. They have but to think of a need and it is fulfilled. Around such people, magical things happen. Around such people, miracles take place.

God Within and We in Spirit Are Ever with You

*D*o not be discouraged about any circumstances. Rather know that your core energy is the God who created all that is. You are the literal temple of God! Therefore, no situation is insurmountable. Don't get caught up in personal emotions, for they are not you. Emotions and thoughts are instruments to be used by you to connect to the earth plane, but you are over and above them both.

You are, deep within your spirit, that quiet, ever-emitting, brilliant white light of peace and love. You need to go into meditation from time to time, if not daily, to dwell there, so that you can vibrate consciously with that core energy that you are and bring it out into your daily life. Then you will not be undone by the appearance of things or by the reality of things in the physical world.

You are on a life path that is being woven into this walk with us, so honor and appreciate this fact. Know that you are created by design to be here on earth, and as we help you in the unfolding of your life, we move right along with you.

Be aware that the spiritual world is the world of *cause* and earth, where your physical body resides, is the world of *effect*. Because this is so, we in spirit who are assigned to you are exceedingly concerned about and interested in the unfolding of your daily life on earth. We desire to participate in your life with you.

In your present life's work or in any activity, we are interested in the right outcome for you. Therefore, you have to know that we are irrefutably bound up in your existence, in the unfolding of your daily life, and in your life as a whole.

This Life Is All about Returning to God

Sometimes you are challenged by life experiences. But it is in overcoming and realizing the deeper meaning of things that we grow, sometimes by leaps and bounds and sometimes by taking baby steps. Whatever the case, life is all about one thing: coming back home to God; returning to God.

Therefore, whenever you are wandering in the darkness, lost in the fog of your mind, or feeling confused or in conflict, just say to yourself, "This is all about returning to God." By doing so, you put your life into proper perspective. Remembering that *this life is all about returning to God* provides God-intended centrality to all that you experience on earth and gives eternal meaning to your existence. Then life makes sense under all circumstances.

The challenges of your life are there—asked for in many cases—so that you can be tested, pass the test, and move higher. That's why we say to embrace all suffering. When you do, it will not kill you; it will reward you with realizations, understanding, higher knowledge, and expanded, wonderful feelings that this life is just as it should be, and you are taking advantage of it.

This moment will never happen again in human history; or this moment, or *this* moment. But all of these moments together are moving you along on a cosmic wave toward the one who created you and gave you life.

Focusing upon God Within

God is light, and there is not a trace of darkness in him. I love this reality! Who would choose darkness over light, if they could feel the all-enveloping reality of the love of God?

I come from that sphere where there is perpetual sunshine. It is a place where God's love shines forth endlessly, abundantly, universally, and we bask in it night and day, in terms of your earthly time. Does that not make you long to go home to God?

This realm is beyond the realms written about in your books on earth. It is beyond your comprehension. And yet, your soul partakes of it perpetually. Otherwise, you could not be alive or exist, as God's being is manifest in your being. Since God is, you are.

Your awareness is possible because of God's ever-present heartbeat and mindfulness within you. Your intelligence—the ability to discern one thing from another, to label things, to comprehend things—is possible because God's intelligence is ever flowing through you. It is an ever-manifesting electrical current of love and light that is the source of all life.

I come to bathe you in that love and light by raising your understanding of just where I come from and where you are headed as you focus upon the reality of God within.

Why Surrender?

*F*irst, you are not this body. You are a soul simply using this body as a means to express. Secondly, you are not your thoughts. If you will notice, your thoughts just come and go without even asking. One moment you have thoughts of anger and the next moment you have thoughts of love. In this way, you could almost say that you are crazy. Third, you are not your feelings. In fact, when you have feelings or thoughts you don't like, you sometimes talk to yourself, admonishing yourself not to think or feel that way.

Who is the individual observing all of this, not wanting to be a part of it? That is your God self or your higher self, the one observing your thoughts, feelings and actions. The more you practice not being attached to anything, the freer you will be from your thoughts, feelings, and actions.

The truth is that for the most part, we are being acted upon and really having little or nothing to say about it. You did not ask to be born in this body; you did not ask to be born to your parents, and so on. Who decided all these things? A force, an intelligence, a personality greater than we are. Therefore, it is better to surrender to that higher power and let it take over our lives.

The Purpose and Goal of Spiritual Practice

You concern yourself with spiritual practices such as certain kinds of prayer, fasting, and religious rituals, valuing consistent adherence to them. We too concern ourselves with these because it is through your consistency in spiritual practices that you grow. However, if such practices become meaningless, your spiritual life will not evolve. If you have certain spiritual practices that you have placed upon yourself or had placed upon you by someone else, such as a church, do them only so long as they retain meaning. Loss of meaning is a sign of their obsolescence. External spiritual practices are all means but often wrongly become ends in themselves. Their proper end is continued evolution to higher and higher forms of spiritual practice until you find yourself totally one with God where all is love.

On Marriage
Before a Live Audience

Saint Germain, could you speak to us about the institution of marriage and the concept of spiritual marriage, as well as your ideas on how two people can form the most perfect union?

I wish I had about three days to answer your question.

[A female member of the audience said, "We can sleep over!" Saint Germain replied, "I cannot!" The audience broke into gales of laughter.]

In any case, all of you spiritually sat forward on your seat when this question about marriage was asked. It is because all of you are contemplating it, or have been through it, or are *through* with it. *[Laughter]*

You came into this world as a single individual and you will leave this world as a single individual. Love, the compelling principle, will determine whether you shall be together with the one whom you have loved on earth when you arrive in the spirit world.

It is important to understand that if you choose to marry, you are consciously choosing to take a path of the highest earthly calling and the possibility of the most fulfilling love of your life.

When experienced at the highest possible level, marital love partakes of the love of God. At the very least, it can imitate God's love, which is unconditional. Planned by God as the supreme path to self-knowledge, it can be, therefore, the most challenging experience in love and, when achieved, the most fulfilling.

When one is truly successful in marital love, such love yields the greatest joy, the highest fulfillment physically and spiritually, and the ultimate experience of heaven on earth. It becomes a spiritual marriage when God is consciously included as dwelling in each, and honored as such in a transcendent love. Then you have a marriage in heaven as well as on earth, and that marriage may continue into eternity.

Spiritual Ascension: Climbing the Mountain of Life
You Can Do It!

We have been labeled Ascended Masters. We laugh from this side at the various and multiple concepts you earthlings have of this lofty title. We are not flattered. If we are ascended, it is the Mountain of Life that we ascended. This in itself should tell you the nature of our ascent.

We are not celestial beings raised from humanity by any other means but by the springboard effect of humility. We practiced, through much trial and error, the presence of God. We stumbled much to find the key. We came to realize that we were, because of God. And this humbled us so greatly that we forsook our previous ideas of life and self and committed our lives to humility before this Great Principle, this Great "I AM," this ever-loving, ever-giving, eternal, glorious, sensitive, tender being whom we call God, and personally, our father. This is the road of an ascended master.

And so you see, we have scaled the heights and plumbed the craggy depths of life's mountainside. And from this side, we continued our climb by helping others up this undeniable Mountain of Life. We have climbed many paths and many cliffs, many sharp and jagged ways in helping others up this mountain. We have repeated, thousands and thousands of times, the same truths. One of the most repeated truths we have whispered in countless, countless spiritual ears is, "You can do it!"

Knowing Yourself

When we talk about knowing yourself, we are not talking about the external reality of your life. The truths that you need to know about yourself are eternal truths about eternal life, and you can find these answers only by going inside. In the deep meditation experience, God speaks to us through us, and the deeper and higher you go in meditation, the more you know that God lives in you. This is a universal truth. God lives in everyone, and not one human soul who has ever lived in the plane of the earth is an exception to this reality. Therefore, dear one, move as quickly as possible away from too much concern about the external world, and center your concerns upon the inner life. As you do that, much guidance and many, many answers for your life will come to you.

God's Love for His Creation

All is a gift of God that he unselfishly shares with us. He is no father who simply wants worship. What is worship after all? Is it not our genuine expression of love and gratitude to the parent who gave us life? Should we not be grateful and express our worship of God at least by an expression of thanks within our hearts? Our love is all that he desires from us. Nothing more! He owns everything, so there is nothing we can give to him that is not already his. The only thing we can give to him that he does not own is our love.

Love is not a bouquet of flowers or an altar covered with fine linen and burning candles. It is not money. All outward efforts to give love are but forms through which to demonstrate or express our love. But they are not love itself.

Because God is love, he knows nothing but giving. It is not in his nature to withhold love any more than water can exist without wetness or light without heat or night without day. God created everything for us. All is given freely to humanity.

It is hard for materialistic human beings to see this reality. It is hard for a man who always seeks a return for his investment to believe God wouldn't. Such people fail to see *love*. Love in its highest expression escapes them. So God goes on looking and looking for those who truly love and appreciate love for love's sake, nothing more, nothing less!

Behind each flower is an energy that keeps it sustained, alive, vital. Behind every form is this life force, real, transcendent, and containing absolute love. God is behind every form. This force, never ceasing, does not relinquish its purpose. It pours forth tirelessly and returns to it source.

Your Light Essence

To overcome the vicissitudes of this life, you need not fight them. All you need to do is turn to the light within yourself. And you do this by inquiry into self.

I, Saint Germain, am able to channel through to you in this way, because as a being of light I synchronize the frequency of my light force with that of Philip Burley.

This light essence, this light that you are, call it soul, Atma, spirit, or whatever name you wish, is unchanged and unaffected by anything, for it is the light of God manifesting as your eternal self. Therefore, when you go within and turn to this illumination that you are, you are turning to an unwavering, unchanging light of love and truth. It is your resting place of absolute stability and understanding.

Beloved ones, you *are* light beings! If you could but see your own light—and you need to see your own light—it would be possible for you to view your own spiritual being. Only ignorance and lack of life experience have kept you from it. But if at this very moment I could open your spiritual eyes, allowing you to see the very reality of yourself, you would stand in absolute awe of the beauty of your soul!

That light can never be shut out, can never go away, can never be removed, for it is that spark which God gave to you from the beginning, and it is the *real* you.

When Anchored in God

While, like you, I can display the full array of human emotions if and when needed, I am never overcome by great fluctuations in my feelings as manifested in moodiness. I am steadfast in my purpose and not moved or swayed by subjective awareness. If you are consistently moved by the spirit of God, mood swings are almost non-existent. Such emotional volatility is more a thing of the earth plane where few understand or embrace an eternal purpose. Lacking this knowledge and dedication, they also lack a strong will to act with consistency. Thus, the awareness of most individuals changes from day to day, resulting in multiple emotional ups and downs and a scattering of precious human energies.

I never change essentially, because I know my eternal purpose and therefore my daily duties. This results in absolute security at all times. My core energies, like those of the father whom I serve, are peace and bliss itself. Anchored in God as I am, I ride upon the waters of his wisdom and bask in the sunlight of his love. Under such conditions, how can I not be totally secure and consistent in all that I do?

All Work Is Holy
Speaking to a Dentist

Entered into fully, your work cannot help but lead you to enlightenment because you were born to awaken to God within through service. Educate yourself in human nature and in the love of human beings. Meditate upon this reality, and when you serve your patients, treat them as yourself, or as God within. Your occupation is among many on earth where you are privileged to repair the human temple or the body. In your practice, you enter a very personal part of the human being where the mouth eats and the tongue speaks. Through this area, the body is nurtured, the temple is maintained, and the individual speaks his or her truth. With the right attitude, your work is not a mundane thing. With the right attitude, and by lifting your mind to heaven, your work suddenly becomes a sacred work, and your office a holy place.

The Magnificent Reality of Self

Each human being is an emanation from the mind of God. Out of his reflecting and pondering, out of his loving and caring, you came to be. He gave birth to you as a soul by projecting your image, through sound and inner visualization, into existence. It was his love for the ideal you—a reflection of his own image—that willed him to bring you into reality.

The ongoing circuitry of God's love flows through you always. God is eternal and infinite, and these two aspects of his nature give you and me our eternal and infinite nature.

By continuing to realize who you really are—God in you; you in God—you have all that you need to go forth and be all you are intended to be. The more that you humble yourself to the reality of which I speak, the more will you come to be your real self, and the more successful will your life become.

For the Love of God I Come

It has been God's endeavor and ours to join hands in this cause of evolving the consciousness of humankind. It has been the effort of God to bring each one of you closer and closer to him. And we in the spirit world are sent to carry out God's effort. Love itself, which God *is*—essentially, most fully, and most emphatically—compels him to do no less.

Therefore, neither I nor those who come from the vibration whence I come are interested in phenomena itself. If you marvel at the fact that I, a mere humble spirit, am coming through another being on earth, then you have missed the point. I come with all of my messages, not to impress you with my appearance, but to bring you into the very presence of God.

It is my most ardent desire for you to hear and feel the truth that I bring so that it may work as salve upon the wounds in your heart. May it work as medicine to take away the spiritual fever, the fears and doubts, and increase your faith, so that you may walk more closely with your real self and God.

Loving Servants

The more you hunger for knowledge of self and the greater your faith to receive that knowledge, the easier it is for your teachers and guides in spirit to help you. We are very, very near wherever you go. I, Saint Germain, and other spirit guides and teachers will always protect you. Depend upon it, and call on us for protection. Demand it, and we will dutifully and lovingly serve you.

Even as many spirits serve you, so they serve me. All the masters are in one long line of servants. We are not glorified in some extravagant way as some people think. Instead, we work as humble servants among you. We follow the great directive of Jesus the Christ in understanding that those who are greatest among you will be servants of all (Luke 9: 47-49). If you would master self, find people whose suffering is equal to or greater than your own and serve them, even if it is only to pray for them. That is the secret to self-mastery, the key to self-mastery, and the path to self-mastery.

Finding God

If there is anything we all need, it is more love, but not from God or others. The love we most need is the love we can give to ourselves. We can love ourselves by doing the right thing in life by going inside and discovering the presence of God, who is already there. We do not have to earn God's presence or love. That is a terrible false teaching. We do not have to go out among the stars to find God. That, too, is a wrong teaching. God is with you as much now as he will ever be. You have only to overcome by letting go of your ignorance and increasing your understanding of this reality. Practice this understanding, and God will come forth from within you.

What Is Self-Mastery?

Learning to direct your thoughts and actions correctly, toward good outcomes, will advance you on the path of self-mastery. Most people in the world today know what is right but don't know how to do what is right. They start out with good intentions, even having a plan of action, but they fail to maintain their focus. They begin by heading in the direction of their goals and then stop or get waylaid.

If we know what is right and good, then of course that is what we should do. Most of us imagine and daydream about what is good, but then cannot make ourselves act on that. Sometimes we become lazy, sometimes we forget to act, and sometimes we become distracted and go off the path.

Self-mastery has to do with directing our thoughts and actions to achieve the right ends, but ultimately it has the most to do with loving correctly. I advise you to love all people as you do yourself, unconditionally. To the person who achieves self-mastery in this way, there are no strangers. When such a person sees another person, he sees himself. Jesus Christ of Nazareth stands out among the greatest of masters because he achieved that kind of love.

To achieve self-mastery, you must have right thinking, right action, and right results. The area of life where that is most essential is in the area of love. Yes, to know in your mind what love is, to act in love, to bring about the right result by loving all people as self—that is self-mastery.

Why Should You Develop Your Spiritual Abilities?

My driving ambition is to help as many people as possible to awaken to their inner spiritual gifts, not necessarily to become channelers or mediums, but so that they may realize their inner powers and use their gifts to help themselves. Many people, for example, could save themselves much suffering if they could read the auras of others. This would help them avoid becoming close to people with whom association might be harmful. There are those who are so sensitive that when they look at their cars, they can detect something wrong with their engines before the car breaks down. In outer space, American astronauts have tried to communicate mind to mind. In any case, there are many practical applications of one's spiritual power, such as discerning mechanical problems, quick communication in emergencies, and crime solving.

Can you imagine a world in which telephones are not necessary? You will not find one telephone or cell phone in the spirit world except in a laboratory where they are trying to bring new inventions to the earth plane. Instead, if we want to communicate with someone and invite that person to meet, we just send out a thought. It reaches the person in the blink of an eye, and the response comes back as fast. What a convenient ability this would be for you! I am speaking at length to inspire you to inspire yourself to develop your spiritual abilities.

In order to be successful, you have to practice, just as you have to study everything you can about any field you are entering. It is most important that you learn how to meditate and pray to be able to communicate quite literally with God within and quite literally with your master teachers and guides in the spirit world. Then the door will open wide for you and you will be most useful to yourself and others in this life.

Patience

One reason you are brought to earth is to learn how to be infinitely patient. Patience is an attribute closer to God's nature than all others. We may say that God is divine love, divine truth, and divine will, but without God's infinite patience, none of the other attributes can exist or be of use. If you can master patience, you can be a master of everything and everyone, and you can be victorious in this life. Patience is the number one virtue, because without it, no ambition can be fulfilled, no matter what it is. Patience and faith are the foundation for the expression of divine truth, divine will, and divine love.

You Are Love Itself

You are born in love. You could not be who you are without that fact. But now you are ready to go to the higher plane of the full realization of mastering love for self first. You are in that process now. From now on, **dear one**, when you look into the mirror, greet yourself as love. **Allow that** reality that is already present in you to come forth. **The more that** we live this way, the more we become what we **think and say.** Doing this will affect your whole life. One who uses **this mantra**, "I am love," reaches the high planes very quickly. **No ritual in the** world can get you to that place unless you obtain **love**.

Many people are searching for **God**. Who is God? Where is God? What is God? From our side, **there** is the obvious awareness that God lives in you. Therefore, if **you** dwell upon this love and say, "I am love itself" over and over, then you will bring both love and God out of you.

You see, dear one, many years have been spent to come to this moment so we could meet. This is your divine destiny; not so you remember Saint Germain, but so you remember that you are love. It is the most important fact of all of your life, and out of it will be born a new you.

Put Your Spiritual Life First

Be sure that you keep your priorities straight. One day you shall step through the veil and meet all of those guides and loved ones who have been giving direction and help to you. You want to be able to face them saying, "I have done my best. I exceeded my highest expectations. I can look at my spiritual character and say to myself, 'Well done. Well done.'"

The dimensions of your spirit—that is, its size and illumination, whether dull or bright—shall be seen immediately by your own eyes when you arrive in the spirit world. All of the environment shall reflect what you have achieved or not achieved in this lifetime. There is no such thing in the spirit world as hiding from the truth, so do not delude yourself by running after the material world at the expense of your spirit. Do not say, "After I obtain my physical attainments I shall begin working on the spiritual aspects of my life." That is completely backward. By going about it that way, you will not draw to yourself blessings and help from the spiritual world to achieve your goals. Put spiritual things first. Then the material world will respond to you positively, and you shall achieve your ends.

The words that I speak are not my opinion but fact based upon my own experience and observations and upon the spiritual laws of life.

God Is Your Beloved

When we become anointed as masters, we are so because we have broken through from theory to fact; from an ideal of God to the reality of God. We know experientially that God lives within.

When that happens, many cry for hours and days because that which they longed for was present all the time while they were searching on the outer plane. I cried endlessly when it happened to me because that which I sought was already mine, yet I had not known it. It is like a man who longs for and misses his beloved, while standing beside her with closed eyes, not knowing she is there. When he opens his eyes and sees her, she is no longer an idea in his mind, and he falls upon her shoulder and embraces her with many tears and with so much love, because he has come home. He has found the love of his life.

This is who and what God is: the love of your life. Many want to make God into some kind of infinite abstract energy, or intellectual power; something outside and beyond human experience. Not true. Not true. God is all of that and more, but at the core, God is your beloved.

We Are All Masters

Saint Germain is more than the sum total of what you are presently experiencing here, and so are you, in the expanded version of yourself. You think of yourself as you see yourself in the mirror, as you conduct your life through whatever work you do, in relation to foods you favor, and so on. You identify yourself with those things. I don't. I identify myself with cosmic thought, cosmic living, and limitless living. I have the ability, as you do, to be multi-faceted. I can express all kinds of emotions, all kinds of thoughts. I can take on all kinds of personalities, if I so desire.

Are you not made in the image and likeness of God? Then look at how many facets there are of God. And if you're going to reach the totality of who you are, you're going to realize that you have many, many characteristics you have not even begun to touch in with, let alone understand.

You need to test [my words] against the backdrop of life experience, but you'll not find them wanting.

I Am Worried Most About My Oldest Son

Your twenty-seven year old son is the victim of being the number one son. We are always harder on the first child because as parents we are, in a way, experimenting. Therefore, first children in the family often have a difficult time being able to feel truly free. Consciously or unconsciously, older children sometimes resent the fact that more is expected of them because they are supposed to set an example for younger children.

When we know what we want to do in life, and we have a very clear vision, we simply step out and go for it. It becomes obvious from our side that your son does not have a vision of his future, and therefore, he is insecure about stepping out. In his heart of hearts, he would like to leave, but because he is not clear about himself and does not have self-confidence, he cannot do so easily. In this insecure position of not having a vision, he becomes defensive.

Belief is energy, and you can help your son by believing in him. If you think of him with disparaging ideas or concerns, that energy will reach him, and it *is* reaching him. Therefore, in your mind and heart, whenever you think of him, think of him as being successful. You can help him best by being very loving and silent, encouraging him whenever you see something good that he does. Have the awareness that your belief, your prayers, and your thoughts have great influence upon him if you hold them steadily.

Each day, in silence and in isolation, sit thinking of him. Use a picture of him if that helps you to do this. First, in your mind, see him as being more secure. See him catching a vision, a clear vision, and in that same effort on your part see him leaving your home, going out, and being happy and successful. Keep repeating this exercise for at least one month. This energy will reach him. This energy will influence him. I have seen many miracles take place by using this method.

In Awe We Worship God, and He Responds in Love and Gratitude

So magnificent are the upper realms of the spiritual world where God manifests most fully, that there are no words to describe them. We are in awe, in pure awe. These feelings of awe are one form of worship, spoken or unspoken. We realize that we have seen with our own eyes and felt with our own hearts that out of the beauty of God's artistry, out of the beauty of his musicianship, out the beauty of his mathematical mind, out of all aspects of his nature and character, are the things of creation expressed. As we appreciate creation as the outer expression of God's inward nature, we appreciate him—that he is greatest, he is the genius of life, he is the source of all.

God appreciates what we are experiencing, and he responds within us to a profound degree, sending us into states of ecstasy with his love and gratitude. It is all so glorious!

64

Spend Time on the Inner Path

You each came here as a direct manifestation of the living God. The message of who you are and what you are to do with your life is written inside of you. This is why the greatest teachers have said, "Know thyself."

You may look at the phenomena of the world and say there is insanity, but there is not a thing you can do about it. If each of you would stop looking at the world and look into yourself and resolve your own insanity, correct your own imperfections, and stay away from newspapers, gossip, and negative talk, the world overnight would become heaven on earth. Do not stray from your own territory. Do not compare your path to another. Do not think that the grass is greener on the other side, but rather relish, appreciate, worship your own life and God within it.

Where is God? He is inside of you. How do you experience God? Through your very self. While angels and spiritual beings such as myself have appeared and given manifestations and done miracles and been seen in our light body, our appearance is the lesser experience. The greater experience is to learn to go inside, to go beyond the layers of what you think is life, of what you think is true, and discover your own God-presence. Sanity will return to each individual as each individual turns to God within. As long as you place God outside of yourself—someone to be reached in spatial time—you will be searching amiss. You will not find God, in the personal sense, except in yourself.

How do you think we masters achieved self-mastery? It was not gained easily. It was not done overnight. Why do you think we teach, "Know thyself"? Why do you think we teach meditation? Why do you think we say over and over, "God is within"?

What is Life without Suffering?

*T*hose who would curse life because there are undulations—because today they are high, tomorrow they are low; today they are on the mountaintop, tomorrow they are in the valley—are unfortunate. Those who would be upset over life's realities do not understand that this is the rhythm of life. The mountaintop and the valley are both there, and all extremes between, to teach us of ourselves. If you embrace both the light and the darkness, and know that both are there for your highest good—by seeking to understand and learn from both—you will grow quickly. When you deny your suffering, that is, when you say life is unfair and unjust, you only lengthen the time you will suffer, or you will cause yourself to recycle through the same negative experience and not spiral upward.

God is the creator of all. Adversities as well as blessings are in your life that through these extremities, and all degrees in between, you come to know who you are. For what is life without struggle?

Fulfilling the Ideal of Marriage
To a young man about to marry

Spiritually, the roundedness of your face is ideal because it spells balance. It is the Buddha face. Therefore, when you look in the mirror, thank God for *you*. Most important, however, is to have a rounded and balanced heart of love. You and your beloved do that for each other, you see, and this will be a very successful match. Part of you has already been listening to the voice within quite closely. Remember this one thing, my son: There is no ideal man or ideal woman. That is why God put the two sexes together so that, as they go through life together, they round out each other. Accept your wife and yourself just as you are. Don't try to change her.

In a true, ideal spiritual marriage, the two do not marry to change the other, but to change themselves, and true love will do that. Marriage is not just for the joy of sexual union. Sex is the least of the concerns. Marriage is more the result of day-to-day endurance toward an ideal. You are a more advanced soul, and we know that you want to pursue the upper path, because you are concerned about your life after this life. When you reach the level where I am and experience the love of God inwardly, there is no parallel. No other love can excel the love of God within us. That is why, when people truly seek the inner path, they forget about their bodies and pursue only God.

Why I Am Called a Master

Because I worked at self-mastery and obtained it, I am called a master. Therefore, I have a considerable awareness of what it is to reach, and exist in, a highly expanded state of consciousness. It is not theory to me. Otherwise, I could not have achieved self-mastery nor could I teach about it, you see.

When I was on earth, most of you know I performed many so-called miracles. You cannot do that simply by being an ordinary person. You have to transcend into that part of yourself where the magic is, where the divine spark is. And consciously, over time, and by the grace of God, you have to release that divine power within you and streaming through you at all times, to perform such so-called miracles.

Because of my entire life experience on earth and here in the spirit world, I am able to go between the Golden Path (the royal path to God) and the lesser paths. Due to full self-mastery, I am equipped to come to you this way by lowering my energies; or I can soar ever higher and higher into the very heart and mind of God.

The Individual Is Most Precious to God

Everyone is looking to win over forces at large. But it is the change of each soul, one by one, that reverses the destructive course of history. If only each of us could realize our value in this way: "I must change, for I am part of the whole, and as I and others change, then the whole is changed." Our individual existence makes up the whole. Without the individual, there is no whole. Therefore, never take yourself or another human being for granted. There is no person who is unimportant or unneeded. All are needed. It is vitally important for each to change concretely so that the abstract whole can change.

The unity of individuals appears as a special beauty for God to behold. Still, it is the unity within the individual that makes it possible for individuals to be united as a whole. Beauty of a united person is first and most important, and unity among individuals is secondary and resultant. Therefore, the individual is most precious to God.

Jesus: A Supreme Example of Self-Transformation

Jesus was unique in history because he learned the art and principle of self-transformation quite early in life. He did not feel self-pity, but empathy for God and others. He learned how to take the negative and make it positive. His whole life course was so guided. Jesus knew how to raise his thoughts to victory, to be triumphant over the evil that sought to destroy him.

This capacity to transform energy is the quality of the Christ within each of us. Christ is but an earthly title to define a prototype—a working model of a man who demonstrated transformation. It is not his crucifixion that makes Jesus unique. It is his transforming possible defeat into victory, keeping his energies focused and raised to God.

Successful people are those who, through mental discipline (self-mastery), habitually transform all of their life energies—good and bad—into victory. All humanity must ultimately gain such self-mastery, applying it moment by moment to achieve victory over the lower self by the higher self. Man must eradicate wrongdoing and evil in the world by starting with himself through self-mastery and self-transformation.

Do That Which Edifies the Soul

*B*eloved one, you have to learn what your own soul is telling you. Many people attend meetings with all kinds of organizations for social reasons, including friendship, and there is nothing wrong with that. Then there are those who go both for friendship *and* to gain higher knowledge, and that is good too. But the larger question is the eternal question: *Am I growing spiritually higher from this experience?* If you answer that you are not, then it is time to look around for something new.

The fundamental way to know whether you are growing is to ask yourself if you are happier and gaining greater peace. Only you can answer those questions. If the answers are no, I am not getting happier and no, I am not getting more peaceful, then you must question whether what you are doing is of value for eternal purposes. A true master always does that which edifies the soul, and he or she leaves those things that do not.

Because our reason for being on earth is to find and live higher and higher truth, then many times we masters live a very lonely life. True self-enlightenment does not come in groups. We may get certain knowledge and certain edifying, loving experiences in groups, but for the actual growth of the soul, we need to be isolated at times. All the great masters went off by themselves. They did this, not because they didn't love people and not because they were negative, but because their experience taught them they needed to be alone to go inside where they could commune uninterrupted with their higher self and God.

On Aging

*I*t's not over until it's over, and there may be some very large good surprises ahead of you. Keep a positive frame of mind, because God works with the positive. Don't look at your body; look at your soul, which is eternally youthful. Dwell there.

It has been said that, I, Saint Germain never aged, and that I discovered the elixir of life. Well, partly that is true, but the greatest elixir is positive thinking. That will keep you younger than all the cream and all the massages in the world. You have to be young from the inside out to be young from the outside in.

The More We Serve, the More We Love

You see, dear ones, before we loved those whom we serve, God our father loved them. Because you are literally God's offspring, there is no burden too heavy for him to bear in helping you. Such is the nature of a parent's heart. Such is the nature of our hearts, who come on his behalf.

The more we serve you, the more we love you, to the point that while there are times you do not need us directly by your side, you are never out of our thoughts. Even if we are off assisting another or at some other needful task in the world, we return quickly when you are in dire need.

True Enlightenment

*B*eloved ones, you will increasingly awaken to that warm, brilliant, blinding, all-encompassing light within yourself. It is shining there now. You have but to open the windows of your understanding to dispel the ignorance that blocks out that brilliant light.

When that light comes in fully and completely, it floods your whole being with all that it is. Therefore, in a moment of that experience, there comes eternal understanding—comprehension beyond any level you have ever aspired to or realized. Then you know yourself as you are known by God and us. The darkness of ignorance that covers the window of understanding is removed from you by the inclusion of this magnificent light, and you see things as they are. You know all things as you tap into endless universal consciousness, and the emanation of God's thought flows unhindered and fully into yours. This is how true enlightenment is made manifest.

The Force of Goodness Behind All of Creation

It is our observation in the spiritual world that masses of people don't have a clue about purpose and are just living randomly from day to day; but if you look at the universe created by God, it is very purposeful. It is ever moving toward the fulfillment of its essential purpose, and there is, among all things within the universe, order.

When we do not have this order in our lives, it means God is not our center. There truly is no center to life unless God is the center. How you know God, how you experience God is your individual path. No one can say to you that God is this or God is that. Since all things came from God, God is everything. There is nothing in which God does not exist. But you will meet God according to your own personality and life experience, and he or she will be as real to you as to anyone who experiences God.

When I speak of God, I speak of goodness. There are many who believe in goodness and the practice of goodness. It is the same as believing in God and practicing love. Essentially, there is no difference. We don't have to always personify God, but we have to know that God is the full force of goodness behind all of creation. That is the important point.

Focus on Eternal Values

Most of a life's accomplishments are forgotten as the life unfolds toward its earthly departure. More and more, as we approach life's transition, we look inward to what we have become. It is this way because what we have *become* is that which we will see upon our arrival into the finer eternal vibrations. We begin to recognize that our earthly life experiences were but circumstances to allow us to see ourselves, to direct ourselves, to master ourselves. The sooner we realize this great spiritual truth, the sooner we can live correctly, and the sooner we can find and maintain the God-given tempo of our being. It is another one of these do-it-now instructions.

Inner Reflection Is Crucial

Some will read our words and speak disparagingly of them because they insist they have no time for reflection, to think upon these weightier things of life. They "simply have no time!" Then we ask, "When *will* they have time for their inner life?" Aren't these people out of control? Isn't life running them? When will they have time to take care of and cultivate an inner world of unity and peace with their creator?

It is recognized, of course, that God is in action too, not just in the reflective, contemplative state. Especially is this so in today's fast-paced world. We do not deny this.

What we say to those who deny themselves time for going inward concerns necessity and limited thinking. You *need* an inner life now! Otherwise, you are avoiding the real you and your real, eternal needs and eternal realities. Unless you reflect, you will never realize the eternal "you" deep inside who needs to be fed with correct thinking and feeling, through which alone you achieve correct actions.

To reflect as recommended—to go inside and search around with the light of honesty—may require adjustments in thinking as well as in our outer life activities. But we say that unless you do all of this for yourself you may never achieve what you were born to achieve on this earth—to fulfill the actual purpose of your earthly walk. All of life's circumstances on earth are placed there for you to overcome by mastering self. You are not to be mastered by the events in the unfolding of life. We must understand all of this even to begin to reflect, prioritize, or act correctly! We must demand of ourselves new thinking modes, new ways of looking at life. When we are unhappy, we must look inside to see if we are unhappy because there is no way out or because of the way that we look at life. Almost always, it is the latter and not the former.

Channeling:
A Means to the Truth

The violet light is around you because you are being guided by me. I have been waiting for some time to get your attention. I want you to find out as much as possible about me so that I can draw closer to help guide you.

I am creating a circle of people around the world today, and it is my responsibility in these latter days to do this. These are not people who are just interested in metaphysical phenomena, but those who truly want to understand spirituality and to grow. That is the vital prerequisite for me to work with someone.

There are many people, as you know, who demonstrate the phenomena of channeling, and often the channeling becomes an end in itself. But channeling itself doesn't matter one whit to me; it just happens to be a means by which I can work on earth to bring the truth.

You Draw to Yourself What You Are

Everything in the cosmos is vibratory, in both your world and ours. Vibrations must be harmonious to exist side by side or together. How then can you draw to yourself anything different from what you are internally? It is impossible. As all things operate by universal, cosmic principles, there can be no faking, no pretense, and no sham. It is our message today to say loudly and clearly: You draw to yourself exactly what you are. If you cry and cry to the heavens but find your prayers unanswered, you must ask yourself the condition of your own heart.

"Ye are gods" means the power of creativity and re-creativity of self belongs to you and is in your hands. To become this *real* self—not the self you pretend to be or parade as an actor to the world, but the *real* self—you must be one hundred percent honest with yourself. We stand to aid you in the confrontation, stage by stage, in dealing with the pains of seeing yourself as you truly are. But unless you go through this process of seeing your true inner self and overcoming, you cannot be transformed. It is not enough to spend time and call it progress. The walk of spiritual faith is not a mere passage of time from one point to another, but rightfully consists of growth through transformation.

Little by little, as you truly face yourself with courage and don't flinch or pull back, and you work systematically upon yourself under the guidance, love, and protection of spirit, your vibration changes; and in this gradual transformation process, you draw to yourself higher and higher levels of success, accomplishments, and rewards.

Your Life on Earth Is Very Precious

*I*t is fortunate, blessed we should say, for you on earth to be still in the physical world. We in spirit cannot act and change as we have spoken. We must return to you on earth to aid and support you; for the gift of life is your physical temple. It is by acting through the physical that the soul's vibration can be changed. When we have passed on, we are devoid of this inner resonance between soul and body. Our energies are diminished and we lack the power to grow closer to God.

Why do we take these hours to write and pass on this information? Because we must let you know, dear reader, how very, very precious is your life on earth. To educate, to inspire, and to urge you forward we speak of the truth we know and have experienced.

Unless you reach your maximum growth on earth according to God's blueprint for you, you will still have to return to earth to complete your spiritual growth. Our job is assisting others to liberate earth that through this understanding heaven may also be liberated. Though you may not understand or agree with all of our words, we would ask you to consider them!

Your Transformation through Positive Thinking

As you have experienced, we do work on your energies. We must enter into your vibration, your holy and sacred self. To do this, a foundation of rapport and trust must be built between us. You worry about failures and downfalls. We look past these to potential. We must or our energies will stagnate at negative and lesser levels. Ours is the specific mission of helping you to raise your focus of thought to success and to embrace positive ideas. Only in this way do we truly elevate your energies. Your predominant thought becomes chief among your many thoughts and compels you unwittingly to dwell where that prevailing thought lies. We work to dominate you with love and service and loving thoughts—positive, uplifting thoughts. And as you see the result of these thoughts in your life and life's energies, you will gravitate more and more toward consistency in thinking and living positively. What else is becoming, or transformation?

By Serving Others, We Parent Them

*T*o support others and help them continue from day to day is to encourage them, to speak of positive possibilities, to point out the path to victory. We must consistently point the way to a positive outcome; we must constantly remind the soul in our care to have faith, to keep going.

In a world so fraught with obstacles, it is difficult for all of you to keep going, to be always positive, and to have unwavering faith. And yet, you must. Otherwise, into what state will your mind fall? Where will you find yourselves on the morrow? It is foolish and a needless waste of time to look back, to repeat mistakes, or to digress in any way!

This is our work. And in serving, we actually parent. We are teacher, doctor, friend, father and mother, all rolled into one. Those who are parents understand that parenting is a constant job. Especially when you love, you do not mind. It is often a heart-rending burden, but nevertheless a happy one. When children leave the nest and the door closes on the last one, there is pain in the heart of the parents. Their burdens may be gone as they have known them, but they will feel lost unless they find new ones to serve—to parent.

Such is our task. We want to remove from the mind the thought that there is something strange or mystical about our presence and assistance. In true love, it is all so natural. Those who have loved another because they are they, and not from duty, will readily understand our state of mind, our state of heart.

Accepting Yourself as You Are

There is nothing wrong with being shy, dear one. Were that more people were quiet instead of always speaking; it would be better in the world. You are one of a kind of people. Those who are not shy are always pushing those who are shy to be involved, but you should feel comfortable with being you.

How can you be something other than what you are? Sometimes parents in their insensitivity push a child, saying things like, "You should do this" or "You should be that." Then there is confusion, because the poor child wants to be who he or she is innately.

So the first and most important thing is to accept yourself just as you are. Do not apologize for being you. Don't feel bad or guilty because you feel shy toward people. Unless we accept ourselves exactly as we are, then spirit can't help us.

You can see that sometimes your shyness blocks you from full realization of yourself; but the more that you focus upon being shy, the shyer you become. Therefore, my advice is to accept yourself exactly as you are, and then see what happens. Whenever you feel too shy about something, do not become upset. Just say to yourself, "I accept myself one hundred percent as I am. I don't care what anyone thinks or says; I have to be me." Then watch what happens.

When we fight something, that thing stays with us. When we accept our problems and ourselves just as they are, they lose power. So the secret to personal overcoming and healing is to accept yourself just as you are. Work within your reality, not someone else's.

Meditation:
The Great Journey Inward to Find Your True Self and God

Today, meditation is greatly emphasized on earth, because that journey inward is the last one humanity will make to discover the cause and purpose of life. This inner journey is necessary and is inspired by God. He is calling out loudly and clearly from within the hearts of all humankind, even those whose lack of awareness dims the shining light within. But in time, they too will be reached.

If you are yearning to find the purpose of life and the cause of suffering, and if God truly dwells on earth in the core of the souls of humankind, how much he wants to be heard and to emerge into the total awareness of humanity. If you search, pulled beyond your control, to find answers, know that he is calling within your own being to do so.

The prodigal son is longing now to come home. The father waiting to meet you has never left the homestead, but rather has been calling out to you from the center of your own being to come home:

Come inward to the light! Hear me already inside of your heart, the home of your being; I am already present and waiting. Search no further. I am here! I am so close you cannot see me. Step back from your state of mind and the emotions that often block your view of me, and then you will see me!

When you do see and experience me with all your faculties of discernment, don't be surprised if you cry in joy and sorrow. Joy because you have at last found the king within the kingdom of your heart and sorry because you have missed me more than human words can say and because you didn't know I was here all the time.

I have spoken to you with all the power at my command. In seasons of sorrow I have cried with you. And sometimes as you thought you spoke to yourself, after the cleansing, you were speaking to me.

At other times when you experienced unspeakable joy you spoke to me thanking me. I heard. I was moved, and leapt within your heart and echoed your joys.

In all of this, between the sorrows and the joys, I have never left you. I have always been here. And I shall never leave you. There is a beautiful land here within your soul of souls. I stay here because love will not let me leave. I am a happy prisoner of love. I wanted it this way, and love compelled me to create you so.

I shall stay here no matter how long it takes to bring you through the gates of your true self. And if I suffer, and I do suffer to stay here, it is all worth it. I dream again and again of your return, and this sustains my heart to stay and stay. I wait with untiring love to see you come home. Don't be long in returning, for it will ease your sorrow and mine to hold you within my eternal, abiding love.

About Philip Burley

Born on Thanksgiving Day, November 23, 1939, in Fort Wayne, Indiana, Philip Burley began having early morning bedside visitations from spirit guides and master teachers at the age of four. In the tradition of many mystics, he felt prompted to pray for others and for the world at this very young age. Philip attributes his spiritual awakening and heightened awareness to his early and ongoing encounters with God and with elevated spiritual beings who have guided him since childhood. His search for God has remained the central focus of his life.

Philip has been a professional medium and trance channeler for more than twenty-one years. He has provided spiritual readings to thousands of individuals and has taught numerous seminars and lectures on the nature of the spirit world. He is a master teacher of the art of meditation and spiritual development. Best known for channeling spiritual master Saint Germain, Philip has demonstrated the gifts of channeling and mediumship to audiences at educational conferences and on radio shows throughout the United States. He produced and hosted "The Inner View—Adventures in Spirit," one of the top call-in shows in the Phoenix area. It drew an audience from around the world through the radio and the Internet. Philip is the author of the books, *To Master Self is to Master Life* and *A Legacy of Love, Volume One: The Return to Mount Shasta and Beyond*, both channeled through Philip by Saint Germain.

Philip lives with his wife Vivien in Phoenix, Arizona and enjoys frequent visits with his three children and seven grandchildren.

About Saint Germain

Historically, Saint Germain lived in the 1700s during the reigns of King Louis XV and King Louis XVI of France. According to some accounts, he was a close associate of King Louis XV and the son of royalty himself. He took his name from an area in France, so the word "Saint" in his name is unrelated to Christian sainthood. He apparently used several different names, and that has made him an elusive figure in history. He may have traveled incognito as a security measure against thievery or bodily injury, a practice of many wealthy people of his day.

Saint Germain was an accomplished musician, poet, and knowledgeable conversationalist who was keenly interested in political and social issues. He was particularly concerned about human freedom. He believed that everyone has the right to a unique relationship with God, and that no one else should be able to dictate what that relationship should be.

Saint Germain is known as an adept because his contemporaries associated him with extraordinary attributes. He was said to be an alchemist who could change base metal into gold, and more than one noblewoman of his time wrote in her journal that he never seemed to age, appearing to look between forty and fifty years old no matter how much time had passed. Some wrote that he could appear and disappear at will.

In my experience, of course, Saint Germain still *does* appear and disappear at will! On one occasion, he came in a flash of light in my room prior to my channeling him the next day. Though I had been calling out to him, I had not asked him to appear. In the beginning of our relationship, he told me that the time would come when I would not be able to tell where

I ended, and he began. For me, it is that way now. He is an ever-present, loving, and encouraging mentor, respectfully guiding and coaching me regarding my work and personal life. Over the course of many years, he has won my absolute trust.

When Saint Germain speaks directly through my vocal cords as I give readings, people tell me that his tremendous compassion and deep understanding of their inner experience have a profound healing effect on them. Mediumistic people who observe me channeling him testify to the brilliant purple light and intense energy of love that emanate from his presence.

Whatever the facts are surrounding his historical birth, life, and death, Saint Germain comes today in spirit as a heavenly advisor who consistently represents God's universal wisdom and love for all human beings.

Sources

*T*he *Wisdom of Saint Germain* is a collection of passages taken from meditation circles, spiritual readings, speaking engagements, and publications by Philip Burley. Excerpts from previous publications have been revised for editorial consistency.

Page

1 **Traveling the River of Life**, Spiritual Reading, Philip Burley, Tokyo, Japan, October 9, 2003.

3 **We All Have Problems**, Spiritual Reading, Philip Burley, Tokyo, Japan, October 3, 2003.

5 **The Highest Truth Is Love**, Spiritual Reading, Philip Burley, Tokyo, Japan, October 14, 2003.

7 **Stay in the Light of Your Life**, Spiritual Reading, Philip Burley, Tokyo, Japan, October 16, 2003.

9 **You Were Born out of Love**, Spiritual Reading, Philip Burley, West Grove, Pennsylvania, 1980s.

11 **Writing and Following Your Book of Life**, Dictated by Saint Germain to Philip Burley, Phoenix, Arizona, 2007.

13 **Live Now**, Spiritual Reading, Philip Burley, Tokyo, Japan, October 7, 2003.

Page

15   **God Within and We in Spirit Are Ever with You**, Teleconference Channeling, Philip Burley, Phoenix, Arizona, April 30, 2007.

17   **This Life Is *All* about Returning to God**, Teleconference Channeling, Philip Burley, Phoenix, Arizona, May 7, 2007.

19   **Focusing upon God Within**, Saint Germain As Channeled Through Philip Burley, *A Legacy of Love, Volume One: The Return to Mount Shasta and Beyond,* Discourse Two, "True Enlightenment," © Philip Burley 2003, 31–2.

21   **Why Surrender?** Spiritual Reading, Philip Burley, Tokyo, Japan, November 22, 2003.

23   **The Purpose and Goal of Spiritual Practice**, Saint Germain Through the Mediumship of Philip Burley, *To Master Self is to Master Life,* Chapter 2, "Rounded Mediumship: The Keys to Good Receiving," © Philip Burley, 1997, 47.

25   **On Marriage**, Saint Germain As Channeled Through Philip Burley, *A Legacy of Love, Volume One: The Return to Mount Shasta and Beyond,* Part Two, "Questions & Answers with Saint Germain," © Philip Burley 2003, 193–4.

27   **Spiritual Ascension: Climbing the Mountain of Life—You Can Do It!** Saint Germain Through the Mediumship of Philip Burley, *To Master Self is to Master Life,* Chapter 9, "Spiritual Ascension: Climbing the Mountain of Life," © Philip Burley, 1997, 100.

29   **Knowing Yourself**, Spiritual Reading, Philip Burley, Tokyo, Japan, November 22, 2003.

31   **God's Love for His Creation**, Saint Germain Through the Mediumship of Philip Burley, *To Master Self is to Master Life,* Chapter 27, "Positive Karma and God's Love for His Creation," © Philip Burley, 1997, 249–50.

Page

33 **Your Light Essence**, Saint Germain As Channeled Through Philip Burley, *A Legacy of Love, Volume One: The Return to Mount Shasta and Beyond,* Discourse Nine, "Weaving God's Tapestry," © Philip Burley 2003, 82–3.

35 **When Anchored in God,** Saint Germain Through the Mediumship of Philip Burley, *To Master Self is to Master Life,* Chapter 21, "Christ-Consciousness," © Philip Burley, 1997, 197–8.

37 **All Work Is Holy**, Spiritual Reading, Philip Burley, Tokyo, Japan, October 9, 2003.

39 **The Magnificent Reality of Self**, Saint Germain As Channeled Through Philip Burley, *A Legacy of Love, Volume One: The Return to Mount Shasta and Beyond,* Discourse Eight, "The Magnificent Reality of Self," © Philip Burley 2003, 7–74.

41 **For the Love of God I Come**, "The Purpose of Saint Germain's Coming," Channeled Through the Mediumship of Philip Burley, Alexandria, Virginia, February 27, 1993.

43 **Loving Servants**, Spiritual Reading, Philip Burley, Tokyo, Japan, October 3, 2003.

45 **Find God**, Spiritual Reading, Philip Burley, Tokyo, Japan, October 3, 2003.

47 **What Is Self-Mastery?** Spiritual Reading, Philip Burley, Tokyo, Japan, October 2003.

49 **Why Should You Develop Your Spiritual Abilities?** Spiritual Reading, Tokyo, Japan, October 2003.

51 **Patience**, Spiritual Reading, Philip Burley, Phoenix, Arizona, December 2007.

53 **You Are Love Itself**, Spiritual Reading, Philip Burley, Tokyo, Japan, October 3, 2003.

Page

55 **Put Your Spiritual Life First**, "Life Experiences," Presentation to a live audience, Philip Burley, West Grove, Pennsylvania, April 10, 1993.

57 **God Is Your Beloved**, *Questions and Answers with the Master*, "What about the Future?" Adventures in Mastery, Philip Burley, 2009.

59 **We Are All Masters**, Saint Germain As Channeled Through Philip Burley, *A Legacy of Love, Volume One: The Return to Mount Shasta and Beyond,* Part Two, Questions & Answers with Saint Germain, "Masters, All," © Philip Burley, 2003, 142–3.

61 **I am Worried Most about my Oldest Son**, Spiritual Reading, Philip Burley, Tokyo, Japan, November 22, 2003.

63 **In Awe We Worship God, and He Responds in Love and Gratitude**, Healing, Meditation and Channeling Circle with Philip Burley, "True Religion Is True Love," Phoenix, Arizona, February 20, 1993.

65 **Spend Time on the Inner Path**, Saint Germain As Channeled Through Philip Burley, *A Legacy of Love, Volume One: The Return to Mount Shasta and Beyond,* Part Two, Questions & Answers with Saint Germain, "Spend Time on the Inner Path," © Philip Burley, 2003, 204–5.

67 **What is Life without Suffering?** Saint Germain As Channeled Through Philip Burley, *A Legacy of Love, Volume One: The Return to Mount Shasta and Beyond,* Discourse Ten, "Life Is Eternal, Cyclic, and Growing," © Philip Burley, 2003, 94.

69 **Fulfilling the Ideal of Marriage**, Spiritual Reading, Philip Burley, Tokyo, Japan, November 21, 2003.

71 **Why I Am Called a Master,** Saint Germain As Channeled Through Philip Burley, *A Legacy of Love, Volume One: The Return to Mount Shasta and Beyond,* Discourse One, "Scaling the Summit— Mount Shasta Wesak Festival," © Philip Burley, 2003, 22–3.

Page

73 **The Individual Is Most Precious to God**, Saint Germain Through the Mediumship of Philip Burley, *To Master Self is to Master Life*, Chapter 23, "Stay the Course with God," © Philip Burley, 1997, 210.

75 **Jesus: A Supreme Example of Self-Transformation**, Saint Germain Through the Mediumship of Philip Burley, *To Master Self is to Master Life*, Chapter 24, "Jesus and the Principle of Transformation," © Philip Burley, 1997, 222–3.

77 **Do That Which Edifies the Soul**, Spiritual Reading, Philip Burley, Tokyo, Japan, November 21, 2003.

79 **On Aging**, "Saint Germain Speaks," Channeled Through Philip Burley, IISIS Conference, Los Angeles, California, October 2, 2008.

81 **The More We Serve, the More We Love**, Saint Germain Through the Mediumship of Philip Burley, *To Master Self is to Master Life*, Chapter 25, "Purify Your Energy through the God Within," © Philip Burley, 1997, 228.

83 **True Enlightenment**, Saint Germain As Channeled Through Philip Burley, *A Legacy of Love, Volume One: The Return to Mount Shasta and Beyond*, Discourse Two, "True Enlightenment," © Philip Burley, 2003, 32.

85 **The Force of Goodness behind All of Creation**, Spiritual Reading, Philip Burley, Phoenix, Arizona, July 30, 1996.

87 **Focus on Eternal Values**, Saint Germain Through the Mediumship of Philip Burley, *To Master Self is to Master Life*, Chapter 15, "Overcoming Limitations by Mastering Your Thoughts," © Philip Burley, 1997, 145.

89 **Inner Reflection Is Crucial**, Saint Germain Through the Mediumship of Philip Burley, *To Master Self is to Master Life*, Chapter 15, "Overcoming Limitations by Mastering Your Thoughts," © Philip Burley, 1997, 146–7.

Page

91 **Channeling: A Means to the Truth**, Spiritual Reading, Philip Burley, Tokyo, Japan, October 15, 2003.

93 **You Draw to Yourself What You Are**, Saint Germain Through the Mediumship of Philip Burley, *To Master Self is to Master Life,* Chapter 16, "Transformation through Prayer and Action," © Philip Burley, 1997, 151–2.

95 **Your Life on Earth Is Very Precious**, Saint Germain Through the Mediumship of Philip Burley, *To Master Self is to Master Life,* Chapter 15, "Transformation through Prayer and Action," © Philip Burley, 1997, 156–7.

97 **Your Transformation through Positive Thinking**, Saint Germain Through the Mediumship of Philip Burley, *To Master Self is to Master Life,* Chapter 23, "Stay the Course With God," © Philip Burley, 1997, 211.

99 **By Serving Others We Parent Them**, Saint Germain Through the Mediumship of Philip Burley, *To Master Self is to Master Life,* Chapter 25, "Purify Your Energy through the God Within," © Philip Burley, 1997, 227–8.

101 **Accepting Yourself as You Are**, Spiritual Reading, Philip Burley, Tokyo, Japan, October 12, 2003.

103 **Meditation: The Great Journey Inward to Find Your True Self and God**, Saint Germain Through the Mediumship of Philip Burley, *To Master Self is to Master Life,* Chapter 14, "Meditation: Man's Journey to Find God Within," © Philip Burley, 1997, 140–1.

Mastery Press, Publishers
Phoenix, Arizona

For general inquiries send an email to *aim.az.hq@gmail.com,* or write to:

Adventures in Mastery, LLC (AIM)
P.O. Box 43548
Phoenix, AZ 85080

To receive information about having a spiritual reading, contact:
readingswithphilipburley@gmail.com